Dedication

This book is dedicated to my mother and father for encouraging me to try new things, for supporting my intellectual and creative talents, and for never allowing me to give up on my dreams.

Acknowledgement

I would like to thank my dear friend, Jeremy Desiderio, for his patience with proofreading and for his constructive criticism. Without him the book would be two thirds written and would be stored as a draft on my computer. I cannot thank my artist, Greg Lynn, enough for his kindness, spontaneity, perseverance, and talent. I have said this before and I will say it again. Without his artwork this book would not have been possible. I would additionally like to extend a necessary thank you to my friend and talented photographer, John Welsh. Thanks for your professionalism, your willingness to accommodate a deadline, your agility at dodging pigeons, and for your computer assistance.

Lastly, I would like to thank my friends for listening to my stories and suggesting I write them down.

I would even like to thank those of you who have heard them more than once but were too kind to tell me. Thanks for your continuous encouragement as I informed you of my progress in my initial phase of writing. You were the momentum that kept me writing. And thanks, to my staff members, for making sure I never forgot anything that happened at the office.

-Amy

Table of Contents

Chapter one: Lessons I learned as a student

Chapter two: Degree, license, now what?

Chapter three: What do the patients think?

Chapter four: Injured on the job

Chapter five: I couldn't make these up if I tried

Chapter six: They want me to influence students?

Chapter seven: The wrong idea (things aren't always
what they appear)

Chapter eight: Lessons they never teach in school

Introduction

So you are reading a book that does not have

diagrams, citations, continuing education advertisements,

job listings, product advertisements, or the word journal

in its title. How does it feel? When I began writing I

wondered who would be interested in reading this piece

of literature. Would it appeal to other physical therapists,

students studying physical therapy, physicians, or patients

who once attended physical therapy? Then I realized that

none of that mattered. What was most important was that

I wrote these stories so others could appreciate them as

well.

I have been a practicing physical therapist for over

a decade. Although I have had my share of challenges

with clinical instructors, physicians, patients, students and insurance companies along the way I would not change anything about the path I have taken. I would definitely not change my decision to be a physical therapist.

Graduate classes and internships taught the skills I needed to begin my career. Experience taught the remainder of the lessons. The field of physical therapy is a rewarding one. It requires compassion, communication, patience, and most importantly a sense of humor.

Chapter one: Lessons I learned as a student

I was twenty four years old when I began studying physical therapy. I enjoyed classes, labs, clinical rotations, and the general process of learning. One semester would focus on memorizing facts. The next semester would integrate the information and apply it to specific patients.

When I began my clinical rotations I wondered, like everyone else in my class, if I knew enough to treat patients. I wondered if I could collect an accurate history. I wondered if I could take and record measurements. I wondered if I would properly assess the patient's deficits. Most importantly, I wondered if I could deliver a safe and effective treatment.

On one rotation I encountered a patient who hyperextended his finger playing basketball. He presented with pain, swelling, decreased flexibility, weakness and an inability to play basketball.

I got out my goniometer and measured the range of motion of his fingers. I measured the circumference of his joints. I tested his grip strength as well as the strength of isolated joints. Next I began treating him. During his first visit I asked if he had any questions for me and he said, "Will I be able to play piano when I am finished with physical therapy?"

Knowing that nothing was fractured, there was no need for surgery, and his deficits were reversible, I said, "Yes." He laughed and said, "That's good, because I cannot play now."

It was then that I realized his doctor suggested he say this. It was then that I realized I was taking my job too seriously. It was then that I decided the importance of a sense of humor while treating patients.

A few days later a high school student showed up for his first treatment. He was a soccer player who tore a ligament in his knee and underwent surgery to have it repaired. I, again, was diligent about measuring swelling, flexibility, strength, and I observed his walking style. I asked questions to determine how this injury and surgery affected his quality of life and we discussed his rehab goals.

I began to inspect his incision and pointed out that they shaved his leg for surgery. I leaned in closer and said, "Judging by the amount of hair that has grown since surgery it must have been 16 days since you were operated on." He was shocked and I believe I gained his confidence. I never told him that his date of surgery was written on his prescription. I never told him how many days sutures were left in the incision. I never told him how long a patient should wait after sutures are removed before starting therapy. I never told him that most athletes wish to return to sport quickly and rarely delay their post-op rehab.

Just when I felt like I was a bit more comfortable with clinical skills and communication skills my next clinical instructor had a new challenge for me. He had just finished scheduling a patient for a physical therapy evaluation. He, too, was a soccer player. He sprained his ankle, saw a physician, and was ready to begin treatment on the same day. My clinical instructor told me I would be performing the evaluation.

He quizzed me before the patient arrived to see what I would ask, what I would measure, and what I had planned for the first treatment. I was glad I could answer all of his questions, and I could tell by the look on his face that he was pleased. I wanted to observe his gait, his balance, his ankle flexibility, the swelling, and his strength. My instructor told me I was ready to meet the patient and I could conduct the evaluation. He said I could not use my hands to take any measurements. I

panicked. How was I going to measure flexibility,

strength, or circumference without using my hands? I

realized he was joking, laughed, and felt my heart beating

in my chest again.

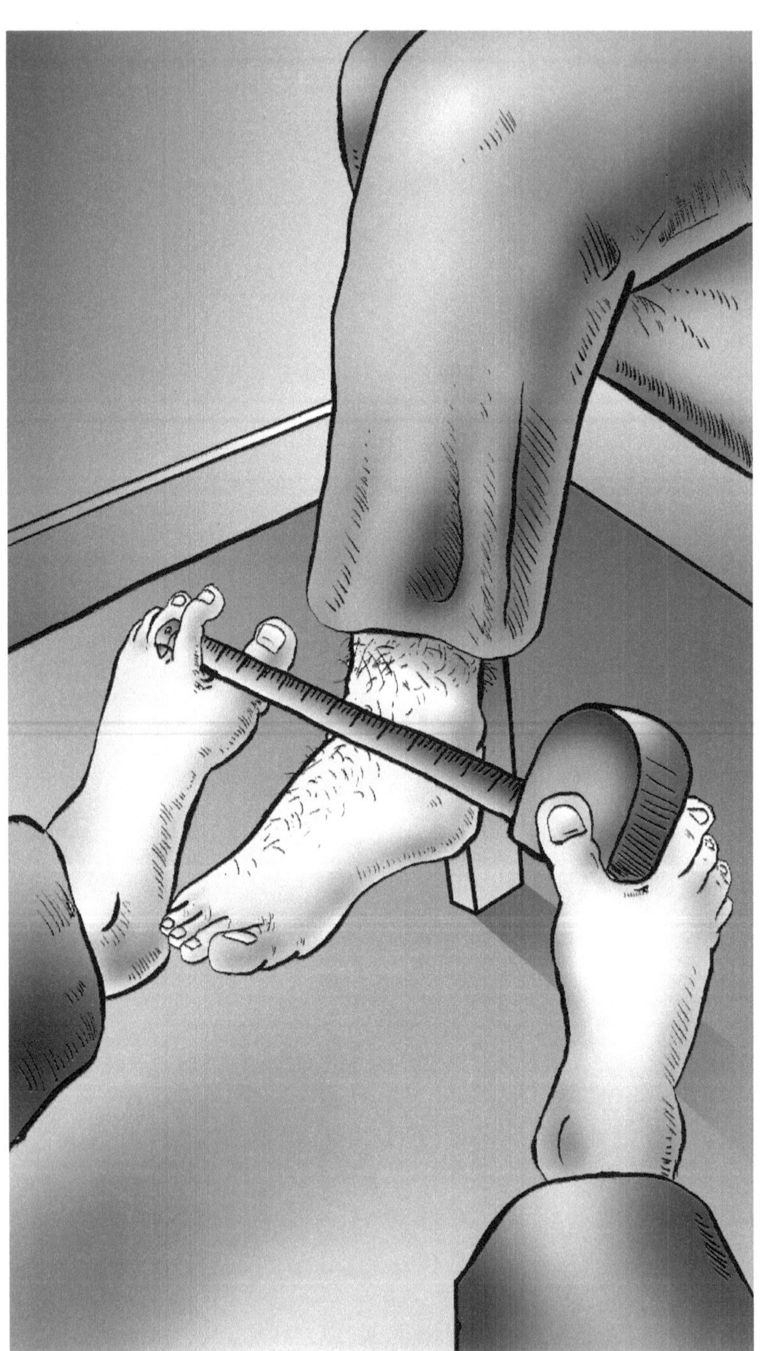

My clinical rotations were not over. Neither were my embarrassing moments. I saw another patient with a torn knee ligament who opted for conservative care and declined surgery. He was a middle aged man who did not participate in sport. He experienced little pain, but complained he felt unstable on his leg. He was motivated to participate in treatment and asked for a home exercise program on his first day.

After I typed his evaluation I left a copy for my clinical instructor to proofread. She graduated from the same school as I, took the same classes, and she enjoyed the job of a mentor. She offered me freedom when I needed it but was readily available if I had questions. Her constructive criticism turned me into a better clinician and it improved my documentation skills as well.

She read my evaluation and asked if I thought my therapy goals were realistic. I did not have a lot of experience writing goals; I had less experience providing the treatment needed to achieve the goals. Nonetheless, I stood by the goals I wrote and said they were appropriate for the patient and were achievable in the allotted time. She continued to question me based on the data I collected, the patient's prior level of function, his willingness to participate in care, his age, and the plan of care I designed.

She had a difficult time keeping a straight face. She thought I had endured enough anguish and asked if I set my goals too high or if I just made a typing error. I apparently omitted the letter "i" when I wrote that my patient would negotiate "stairs" before he was discharged.

I thought that was my last embarrassing moment

as a student clinician only to find it was not. I was told

the night before the diagnoses of new patients on the next

day's schedule. This allowed me the evening to review

anything pertaining to that diagnosis before I evaluated

the patient. It allowed me to review the anatomy,

common subjective complaints, special tests to perform

on the evaluation, as well as recommended treatments.

One day I was told my next day patient had the

diagnosis of Reflex Sympathetic Dystrophy (RSD). I was

excited to see a patient with a less common diagnosis

than prior days. Once I reviewed my notes and textbooks

I was familiar with its presentation, patients' subjective

complaints, and the recommended treatment modalities. I

was ready to establish a rapport, collect data, and begin

treating this patient.

I was not prepared to see her in a motorized

wheelchair. My mind went blank. I did not know where

to begin after I introduced myself. I did not know if she

was in the chair due to the recent onset of RSD or she

was in the chair prior to her injury. The wheelchair

alerted me to lower extremity weakness. The fact it was a

power chair alerted me to upper extremity weakness.

I began history taking, while simultaneously

making note of what I wanted to measure. My line of

questioning was as organized as billiard balls after a

confident break; it was scattered in all directions. My

clinical instructor was nearby listening attentively as I

proceeded. I was trying to determine the nature of her

diagnosis, her pain levels, and her functional ability.

I wanted to keep my questions casual and less

medical. At one point I was trying to determine the level

of assistance and independence she had with her activities

of daily living. I wanted to avoid medical jargon and

decided not to ask about bed mobility. I decided against asking about her ability to roll supine to left sidelying, roll left sidelying to sit, and perform a sit to stand transfer at the edge of her bed. Instead, I paraphrased these skills and asked the patient, "So how are you in bed?"

I have not made that same mistake since.

Chapter two: Degree, license, now what?

There were no teachers or clinical instructors at my first job. There were no other therapists there either. I saw a patient who got injured at work. He tore muscles in his dominant arm and was referred to physical therapy after they were surgically repaired.

I realized the need for scar massage and soft tissue mobilization. I realized the need for modalities for pain relief. I took measurements of his flexibility, his strength, and had him rate his pain. I asked questions to ascertain his functional ability. I learned that this thirty two year old man was having difficulty dribbling a basketball, scrubbing his bathroom, and opening his first beer.

I wondered if I could write a functional goal around opening an alcoholic beverage in his medical chart. Would an insurance company question this? Then I realized I was more interested in knowing why the first beer was a problem but not the remaining ones. I asked the patient and he told me after laughing, "The alcohol in the first beer I drank numbed the pain."

After several treatments of physical therapy I sat down with this patient and evaluated his progress. I measured his flexibility, his strength, his pain rating, and I asked questions to determine if he achieved his therapy goals. Motion and strength were improved, pain was less, and he made functional progress. The patient was now able to type longer, dribble a basketball, and open his first beer without any pain in his arm. He had not, in several weeks, cleaned his bathroom.

Another young gentleman came into the clinic for a physical therapy evaluation. I looked on the prescription and saw the word pain preceded by a body part. Chest pain. So here I am with a twenty year old young man with a diagnosis of chest pain.

He was a muscular gentleman in no acute distress. He had no prior medical history. He denied shortness of breath, jaw pain, nausea, and arm pain. Pulse, blood pressure, and skin color were normal. He was not running a fever. During my history taking I asked if he experienced any recent injuries, accidents, or traumas. He denied all of these.

I observed his neck motion, his shoulder motion, his trunk motion, and I measured his strength. I eventually pressed along his chest muscles and his individual ribs. He said, "That's it! That's where it hurts. That's where the weight bar landed on me when I was bench pressing my last set."

I am no Arnold Schwarzenegger but I know that the act of bench press not only involves lifting a bar off of your chest. It involves preventing it from falling on your chest as well. I am not Webster but I would say that in the event said bar lands on your chest and you are unable to gather enough strength to push it away that this

would constitute an injury. This is especially true if you

need to seek medical attention afterwards.

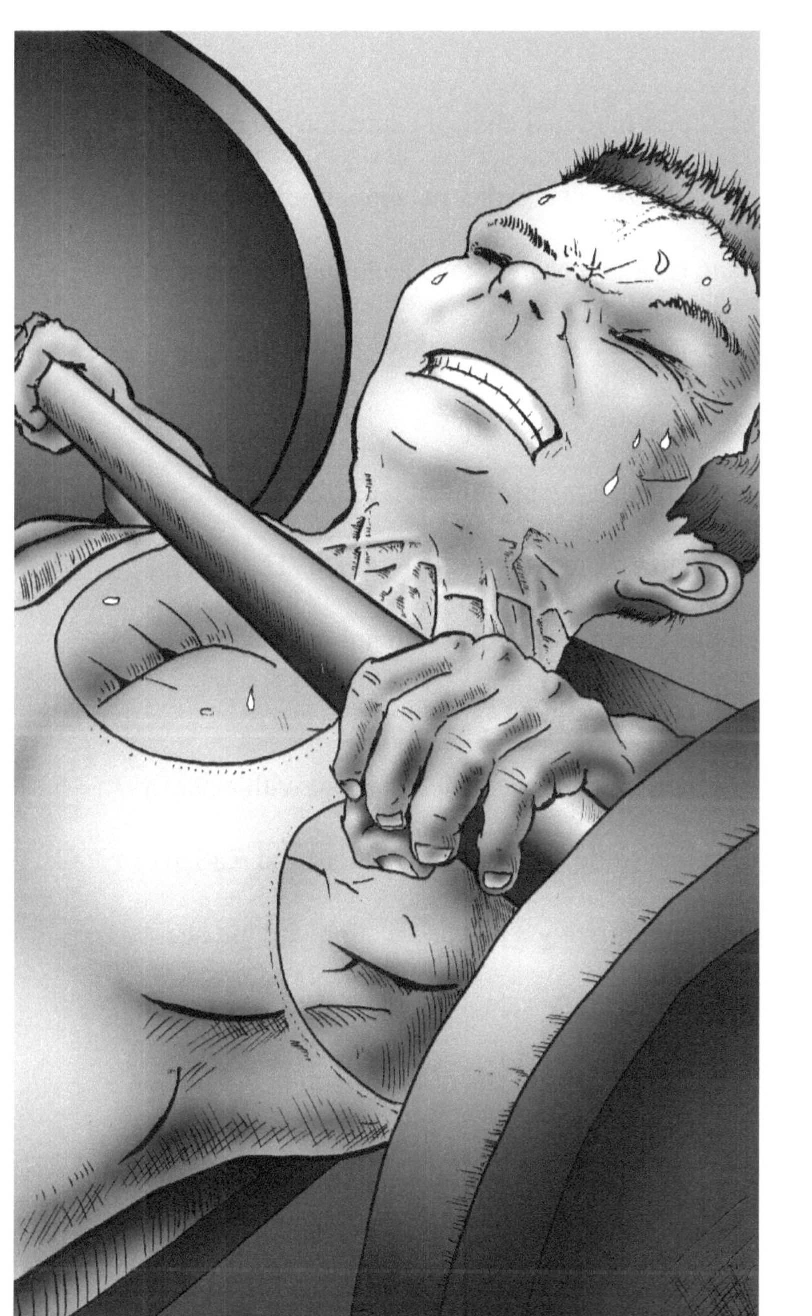

My classroom and clinical education taught me how to speak to patients, gather data in a scientific manner, and treat in a professional and effective manner. It did not prepare me for every scenario I would encounter with patients and referring doctors.

I was in a hospital setting and received an order off a fax machine from a hospital physician. The order contained the patient's name, room number, diagnosis, and therapy order. Evaluate and gait train.

I headed towards the patient's room with a pen, a clipboard, and a smile. I greeted my patient and realized she was not only missing a pen and a clipboard but she was also missing a smile. Then I noticed she had casts on both of her legs. The diagnosis of heel fracture did not mention both feet. I gathered the patient's history, mentioned that her physician ordered therapy, and that after a brief consult with him I would return to begin her first treatment.

I left her room and reviewed all the assistive devices I learned about in school. I wondered if there was one that was not coming to mind. She was not an appropriate candidate for a cane, a four point cane, crutches, or a walker. And yet her script specifically said gait train. How was she to navigate the 9X9 hospital room let alone the hospital corridor?

Gait train? Non weight bearing? On both feet? Was this a practical joke? So I paged the referring physician, introduced myself, apologized for taking up his time, and asked for clarification of his orders for the patient. He realized he erred and said he meant to write, "out of bed transfer to chair." He also agreed to retype the order and fax it to my attention as quickly as possible. Ah, much better. That was doable.

Or so I thought. Did you ever wonder how a patient came to the hospital with fractures on both her feet? Sure, she mentioned during the evaluation she sustained them after a fall. She neglected to say from how high.

So there I was telling this patient who attempted suicide that she was going to remain in the casts for weeks and that her physician did not want her to place any weight on her feet. My next challenge was convincing her of the importance of sitting in a chair,

upright, for a few hours. A woman who did not care for

life hours ago was less interested in doing what was best

for her now.

Chapter three: What do the patients think?

I was continuing to learn about the body, how to interact with patients, and how to communicate with doctors. I went through a phase where I'd started to pay more attention to the vocabulary and body language of patients, staff, and referring physicians.

I trained my aides to prepare moist heat, cold packs, and place electrical stimulation electrodes on patients. They were not permitted to operate the machines. One morning I was catching up on paperwork and an aide came up to me and said, "John is behind curtain two. Can you turn him on?" I giggled silently and began walking towards curtain two. Several days later I heard another aide say, "Mary is behind curtain one. She's waiting to be turned on."

ON
OFF

Whether it was my love of semantics or my fear of sexual harassment, I pulled my aides aside and corrected their choice of words. In the future I suggested they say, "Their *stim units* needed to be turned on."

I always wondered what patients thought when they saw other patients exercising. Their full names, diagnoses, and medical histories were kept confidential by staff members. That never stopped patients from wanting to know more. Nor did it stop them from asking.

I, again, giggled silently when patients spoke to one another. They asked questions I imagined prisoners would ask of one another. "What are you in for?" "How long have you been in here?" "Any idea when you'll be free to go?"

There was one question that a patient asked that turned my silent laugh into an audible one. A young boy was riding a stationery bike next to an attractive middle-

aged woman. He was making conversation to pass the

time. Like most children he was curious and wanted to

know what she had injured. When asked how she got hurt

she said she broke her ankle while walking to work

wearing stilettos. He said, "What kind of work do you

do?"

Chapter four: Injuries on the job

A book about physical therapy would not be complete if it didn't contain stories about people injured while performing job related duties and the rehab required to get them back to work. Now I assure you there will be no mention of symptom magnification behavior in this chapter.

I was told one day that a professional ice skater would be treating in our clinic and she was placed on my schedule. I saw the prescription with groin pull as the diagnosis. After a thorough assessment I decided to begin her treatment with moderate exercise in a pain free manner. I intended to end her treatment with massage, stretching, and modalities.

She was motivated to participate and came dressed in a sweat suit. On her first piece of cardio equipment she removed the sweatshirt to reveal a sports bra. On the second piece of cardio equipment she removed her sweat pants to reveal a pair of petite and fitted shorts. My coworker pulled me aside, jokingly, and said I should be cautious about putting her on another piece of equipment for fear she remove another article of clothing.

Several weeks had gone by and my male coworker was evaluating a patient who was also injured at work. She was a pole dancer who sustained an ankle fracture and required surgery to repair it. After evaluating her he set up a detailed plan of care for restoring her range of motion, strength, and balance. At the end of her treatment he was measuring her progress and I asked if he was going to assess her ability, in detail, for return to work. After all, patients who sustain an injury at work are treated in physical therapy. At the end of their treatment the therapist measures range of motion, strength, balance, and functional progress. The therapist then assesses whether or not the patient can perform all work duties needed for return to work. Did he intend to have her perform a pole dance before he discharged her?

I was treating a patient one day who was reserved and quiet. He spoke infrequently with our receptionist and was not expressive during his treatments with me. He tore his bicep muscle at its insertion and required surgery to fix it. He arrived in my clinic and I explained the severity of his injury, the need to protect his surgical repair, and the complexity of his rehab. He was compliant with his therapy appointments, had great tolerance for manual treatment, and was performing his home exercises daily. He progressed quickly with range of motion and strength gains.

In the middle of his rehab I received a phone call from my secretary. She was sitting at her front desk behind her sliding glass door. She said, "Amy, your ten o'clock patient has arrived. He is sitting down and has a hammer in his hand. What do you suggest I do? Should I send him back or tell him to put it in his car?" I thanked her for the phone call, said it was okay for him to come back for treatment, and I assured her he was not going to hurt me. I informed her I wanted him to bring a hammer in for treatment so that I could teach him supination and pronation exercises for his home exercise program. Some doctors have detected that patients who are injured on the job do not usually like their boss, their job, their reimbursement, their commute, their wives, etc. To date, no evidence exists showing their dislike of physical therapists.

Chapter five: I couldn't make these up if I tried

I remember loving my career while I was working in a soccer clinic. I treated a very athletic population and my patients wanted to get better quickly. They did everything they were told. They scheduled their therapy appointments at the recommended frequency, they refrained from playing sport, they took the medications prescribed by their doctors, and they participated in their home exercise programs.

One young student presented with knee pain and significant swelling. He was treated in the clinic for his first appointment. At the end of the visit he received an ice treatment and was advised to ice twice daily at home. He was informed to place a bag of frozen peas on his knee for ten to fifteen minutes to help reduce the swelling. He was told to avoid sport and keep his walking to a minimum.

Two days later he returned to the clinic. He was

sore and his knee was swollen. He denied playing sport,

and he said he did not walk a lot since his last

appointment. When I asked if he iced his knee he

revealed that he tried but he was not successful. He said

he got a bag of frozen peas from his freezer, opened the

bag, and placed the peas on his knee. He then told me that

the peas kept rolling off of his knee. I waited, silently, to

see if he was joking. He was not.

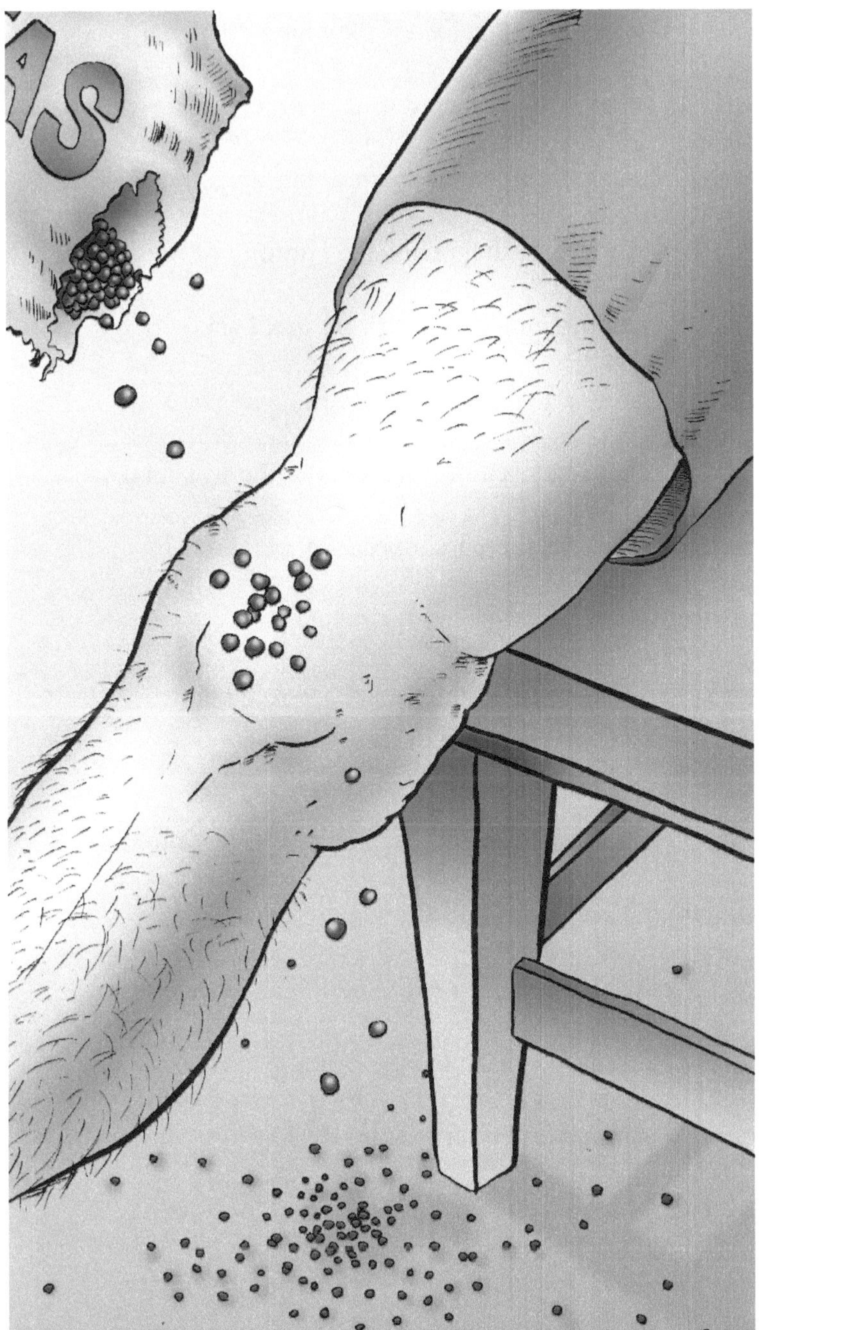
AS

Several years later I believe I may have treated a relative of his. A woman presented in the clinic with complaints of headaches and neck pain. After an evaluation I explained her diagnosis, the etiology of her conditions, the recommended plan of care and I asked if she had any questions. I additionally asked if she were willing to begin her treatment the same day. She was glad to be receiving care and she had hopes of experiencing fewer headaches.

I explained that the first treatment would begin with heat, electrical stimulation, and massage to her neck and shoulder muscles. I educated her on the application of electrical stimulation electrodes, the way they worked, and what she expected to feel. I explained the massage would be done directly on skin using a fragrance free lotion and that she may experience mild discomfort while some of the chronic muscle tension was being loosened. I handed my patient a treatment gown, set up her table with a prone pillow, and said I would leave the room to give her privacy. I explained she should remove everything she was wearing above her belt, cover her front with the gown, and lie on her stomach.

In a few minutes I asked for permission to enter the room. There was no indication during the evaluation that she had difficulty understanding me. The sight I saw entering the room proved contrary. I have seen patients lying face up instead of face down. I have seen patients place the gown on backwards. Until this day I had not seen a patient don the treatment gown on *top* of their clothing.

I was treating a pleasant elderly woman with foot drop. Her exercise routine was designed to strengthen her ankle muscles, improve her leg strength and address her balance. She was adamant about refusing to wear a leg brace. She was determined to perform any exercise that I thought would help her. She also looked at her therapy sessions as a way to socialize with other people in the community. Her routine began with a warm up on a treadmill and she was encouraged to pick up her foot and drop it with as little noise as possible. She continued her exercise routine on a recumbent bike. However, she told others that she was using an *incumbent* bike. Was that because it was the same bike that she had used for her last 4 treatments?

One additional memory I have was an evaluation of a patient with neck pain. She presented with pain, stiffness and was unable to turn her head to her left side. She had only been experiencing this a few days but decided it interfered with all her daily activities and she needed immediate attention. I wanted to determine the severity of her condition and asked about referred pain. I was anticipating an increased sensitivity in her shoulder and upper arm. Instead, she said when she turned her head to the left or bent it forward she felt pain in her cervix. Now that's an unusual referral pattern! I asked her to point to where she felt the discomfort and was relieved when she pointed to her *cervical spine*.

Chapter six: They want me to influence students?

I was fortunate to have had very good professors and wonderful clinical instructors. All were educated, passionate about the field, and enjoyed teaching. They paid attention to subject matter detail, monitored safety, and knew how to provide constructive criticism in an effective and delicate manner.

One day my boss informed me I would be a clinical instructor for a student. I experienced mixed emotions. On the one hand I anticipated being a mentor. On the other hand I wondered if I knew enough to teach a student.

My first student was a young female on her first clinical rotation. On her first day I gave her a tour of the facility, introduced her to staff members, educated her on the hours of clinic, explained the schedule, and instructed her on the format of the charts. I also made it known that any time she had questions that I was approachable.

I asked her what classes she took, how she liked them, and what classes she had scheduled for the following year. I was hoping to place her at ease by asking questions she could answer. I was also gauging her knowledge base to date. I learned that she completed anatomy, medical terminology, modalities, and documentation classes.

We discussed patients together on the first day of treatment. She became comfortable reading evaluations and daily notes and began documenting treatments with accurate parameters in her first week. She observed as I performed the first few evaluations. She then performed evaluations while I observed.

After she evaluated her first patient I suggested we discuss her findings, her clinical assessment, and the treatment plan she anticipated. She decided that her patient with neck pain would benefit from cervical traction so I asked what parameters she intended to use for the first treatment. She answered automatically, without hesitation, that she would use 100 pounds of force for ten to fifteen minutes and the delivery would be a continuous setting. I asked that she pause and give her parameters some more thought; I reminded her that she was delivering the traction to the patient's neck and not to her back. I asked her to think about what she was trying to achieve and whether the parameters were the best ones to achieve her desired goal.

She mechanically delivered a response saying that she wanted to reduce muscle spasms, provide vertebral separation, and reduce pressure on the discs. It was as though a computer was speaking. She did not see the point I was attempting to make. The computer program had a glitch.

I asked her to justify her decision to use 100 pounds of force. I was hoping she would realize this was the amount of force used to begin traction in a patient with back pain and exceeded the amount needed for a patient with neck pain. She simply said, "It was the number I learned in school."

I could have asked her to review her class notes or provide a reference but I instead asked her to estimate the weight of a human head. I asked her how much force would be needed to gently pull but not decapitate the patient.

Several months later I was assigned my second student from the same university. I began the orientation similarly. I asked which classes the student completed prior to this rotation and what her goals for the clinical were.

We treated patient simultaneously initially. She heard my evaluations, read my reports, and she watched as I wrote my daily notes. On a day where patient attendance was minimal I decided to review posture analysis with her. I borrowed a willing employee to pose for a detailed analysis and apologized for any complex my student would give him. I suggested my student look at this staff member from all angles, to write things down, to remove the staff member's shirt to see better, and to feel bony landmarks as needed. She did none of those things. Without hesitation she stated, "He has poor posture." I waited for her to qualify her statement with objective details. I waited to no avail. This student completed one year of a graduate level education, paid thousands of dollars for tuition and texts, and came away with something my mother could have said.

I continued to mentor students. I continued to receive more students. I continued to look forward to going into the clinic each day, and I maintained a sense of humor. With my next student I evaluated a patient with chronic foot pain that was reported at the heel and arch.

The name given to the patient's diagnosis was plantar

fasciitis. My student listened as I took the patient's

history, watched as I took flexibility measurements of the

patient's hips, knees, and ankles, and hovered as I

palpated the patient's arch and heel.

She looked excited to see all the details I collected

were similar to those she read in a school text. The

history, symptoms, and plan of care followed everything

she learned in lecture. She had the look of a child who

opened their gift box on Christmas day and was elated to

find the exact toy she asked Santa to bring her. This

patient made for an easy diagnosis, easy treatment and

easy assessment on progress.

I instructed my patient to lie on his stomach and

asked for permission to initiate treatment. I began

massaging the patient's foot at his toes and slowly made

my way towards his heel. I keep his foot flexed and used

a firm and deliberate massage technique. I stopped intermittently to ask if he was okay with the amount of pressure I was applying. He consented to my handling.

What happened next was no longer text book case. I asked my patient how old his son was. The reaction on my student's face was no longer one of excitement as expressed by the child who received their anticipated Christmas gift. It was, instead, the confused look of a child who opened a gift of potpourri when she expected a toy.

My patient was also a bit confused. He lay silently on his stomach with his head down while I was massaging his arch. But this question caused him to lift his head and turn to look at me the way a grazing deer does when it senses someone approach. It is a look of curiosity but not of fear.

Did he think I gathered this information from his

foot? Was there more to reflexology than its connection

to the body's organs? Or was I a psychic therapist?

He told me that his son was five years old, and he asked how I knew he had children, let alone a son. I confessed that I saw the band aid on his calf muscle with the Spiderman design and assumed he had long outgrown them several years ago.

Chapter seven: The wrong idea

I worked one year in a small physical therapy center with the assistance of one physical therapy aide. He was a high school student who lived in the neighborhood. He was looking for a job to earn spending money and was also considering a career in the medical field. He was personally motivated in learning anatomy, transfer techniques, and modalities since one of his close friends sustained a spinal cord trauma.

My aide and I worked well together. He was proficient with scheduling patients and following through when they failed to attend their appointments. He assisted with the application and removal of modalities. He often asked questions just for the sake of learning; he knew he was not licensed to deliver care.

I was treating a woman who had recently been involved in a car accident. She presented with neck and upper back pain and was unable to care for her three children as a result. On her first treatment I began a soft tissue massage of the muscles in her neck, her shoulders, her upper back, and underneath her shoulder blades. When my hands were placed in between her should blades and I applied pressure, she said, "Oh, right there. That's it. That's the spot." I continued to massage her and she continued to offer feedback on pressure, location and techniques.

I completed massage work for the day, gave her privacy to change, and recommended she schedule additional appointments for the week. Based on her comments my aide asked me what I was doing when we were behind closed curtains.

I worked in the same building as a primary care physician. He heard that I was a talented therapist and patients were responding quickly to their treatments. He saw patients were returning to their active lifestyles and were recommending that friends, relatives, and neighbors schedule appointments in my clinic.

This physician traveled abroad. He retuned with neck pain after spending hours on a plane, sleeping in an unfamiliar bed, and toting luggage. He said medications did not alleviate the pain and stiffness in his neck and he was frustrated by his inability to turn his head to the left. He was unable to drive and when he evaluated patients he would wince if he needed to tilt his head to examine them. On the suggestion of a patient he decided to approach me and ask for help.

He entered my clinic while I was in between patients and I evaluated him. I asked for permission to treat him and asked him to remove his shirt. He, too, had a break in his schedule and had time for modalities. He carefully placed his clothing on the chair in the room, so as not to wrinkle them for the remainder of his shift. I began my treatment with therapeutic ultrasound to a trigger point, proceeded to massage his neck, and completed with joint mobilizations to his neck. He stood, dressed, turned his head, and said he felt seventy five per cent improved.

The following day he returned for a second treatment. We arranged this for lunch break when neither of us had patients scheduled. He walked into the clinic, took off his lab coat and placed it on the first chair. He removed his tie as he walked further into the clinic and it served as a small table cloth for the treatment plinth. His dress shirt was carefully placed on the next treatment table along with his keys, wallet, and pager. It's a good thing that patients did not arrive early to see this trail of clothing.

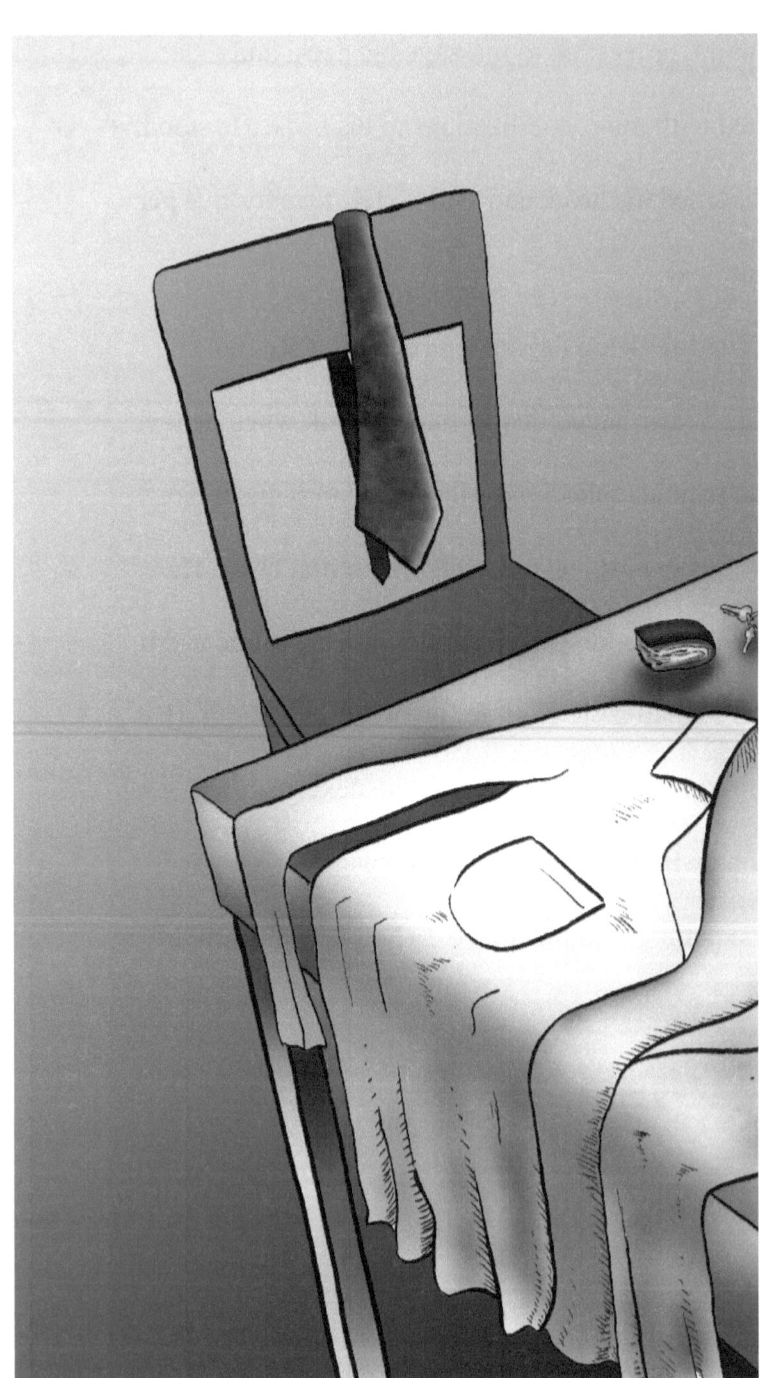

I was working in a clinic in Pennsylvania which saw patients from a variety of backgrounds. One patient who attended treatment was fluent in Spanish. He neither spoke nor understood English. As a result I was forced to recall my high school Spanish education. I knew barely enough Spanish to ask about the nature of his injury, obtain consent to treat, and educate therapeutic exercises. I knew enough for him to schedule with me for his next few treatments.

After several sessions he asked me, "¿Esta casada?" I replied, "No, dorme bien." I translated his original question to, "Are you tired?" I answered, with "No, I slept well." The look on his face was one of confusion. So we continued speaking in Spanish to clarify his question and my answer. As most people who are not fluent in a language have done, we spoke slower, louder, with synonyms a four year old would understand, and with hand gestures. It was then that I realized the verbs "to marry" and "to tire" differ only by one letter. He was asking if I were married and I responded, "No, I slept well." It was briefly embarrassing and we were able to clarify the confusion within one treatment. I am glad he didn't present in a wheelchair so I'd have to ask about his bed mobility in Spanish.

As though the field of physical therapy isn't challenging enough, language barriers add one more challenge to my job. Covering shifts in a second facility on weekends adds another dimension as well. Weekend support staff is usually minimal, and I am unfamiliar with patients as I am not their primary therapist.

Learning the patient names, their diagnoses, prior treatment modalities, and methods of documentation are all important details. Juggling multiple patients at one time and appearing confident is a great challenge. Reaching for a soundhead of an ultrasound unit in a patient's room and realizing there is no conducting gel nearby makes the shift more interesting. This has taught me the valuable lesson that support staff often know more about a facility than the clinician. I recall asking an aide if he knew where the ultrasound gel was and he informed me, "in the documentation room." He said it so nonchalantly that he implied 1) that's where it is always kept and 2) where else would you expect it to be?

I was immediately grateful for the information, thanked him, and proceeded with the eight minute treatment. Moving a soundhead over a body part in slow and circular motions has in the past had hypnotic effects. This time I was more interested in knowing why the gel was in the documentation room. Were treatments conducted in this room containing only chairs and computers? Was the gel used to write notes? Did therapists in this clinic master the art of multitasking? Were they able to write notes while treating patients?

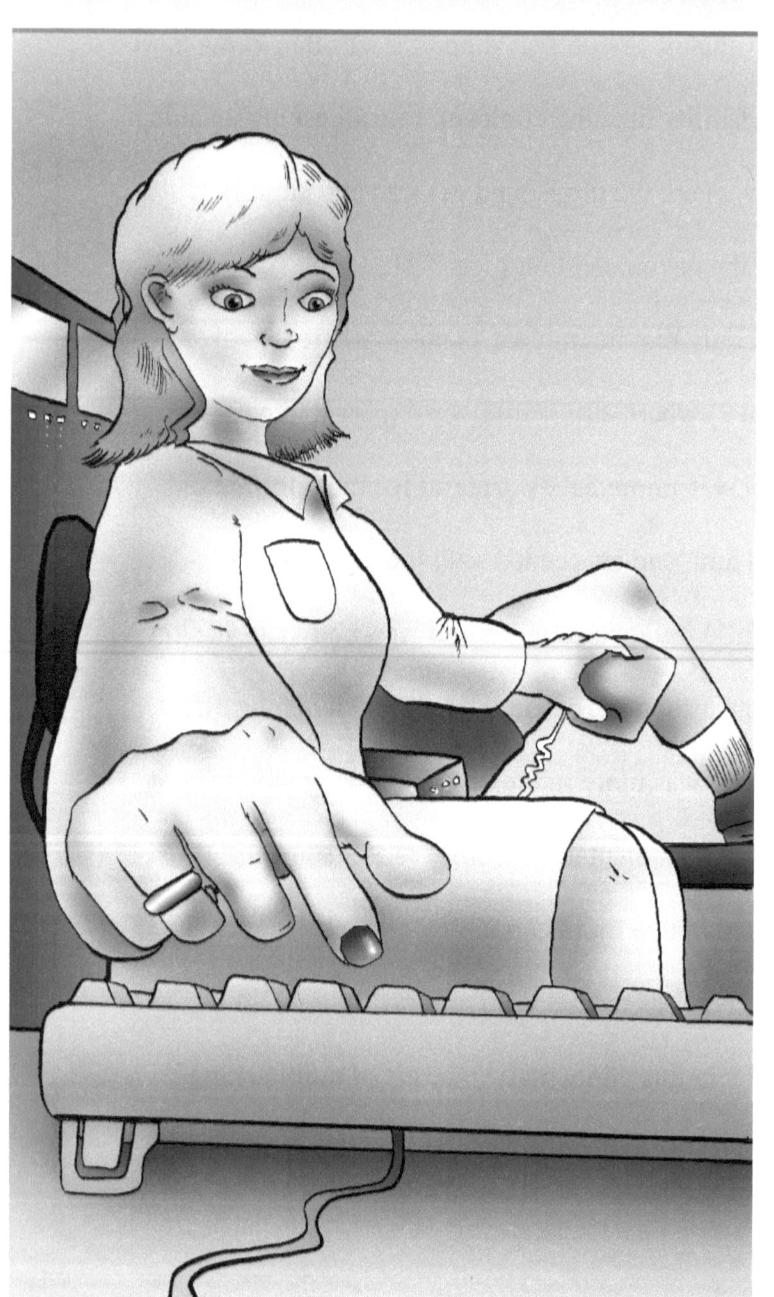

I remember my job search immediately out of school. It was challenging to get a job without experience. People have often had the same difficulty getting a credit card without prior credit. It leaves us with the frustrating thought of how do I begin? That became my opening line. I advertised myself on my lack of experience but willingness to learn. Shortly after changing my cover letter I had my first phone interview. It went well enough that it led to my first interview. The facility advertised that they were a land and aquatic center and successfully rehabilitated patients.

I knew I was qualified for this position. Not only did I learn land and water based rehab in school, but I had spent a year as an aide in a similar setting before I went to graduate school. I was intimately familiar with the principles of water and the effect they had on an exercise program. I was comfortable transferring patients in and out of water, was able to measure their vitals while exercising, and had my racerback bathing suit ready in case there was a need to perform treatments in the water.

When I arrived at my interview location I was prepared. I had a resume, references, my salary requirement, and a few questions about the clinic's schedule and staff. I was escorted into a conference room and remained there for the majority of the interview. I met the clinic manager, the remaining staff, and was then given a tour. I was shown the reception area, locker rooms, private treatment rooms, the gym, and was returned to the room to discuss my start date.

Before going into detail the manager asked if I had any questions and I asked where the pool was. I let him know I was under the impression the facility offered land and aquatic rehab. He escorted me into a room and showed me an empty shower. He explained a patient would enter and it would fill with water. That is where they conducted their aquatherapy. I expected a pool. I expected a pool that a patient could wear a flotation device around their body while performing exercises. I expected one with ropes, lap lanes, and steps. Or at least one that had room for two people. I did not anticipate that something that looks like a shower doubled as a place for a patient to perform their exercise program.

I once treated a woman with an acute onset of low back pain and she was complaining of numbness in her leg. The diagnostic test ordered by her physician revealed that she herniated a disc in her back. She failed to see relief with medications and spinal injections. Her doctor referred her to me for physical therapy.

Initial treatments focused on decreasing her muscle spasms, increasing her flexibility, and improving her core muscle strength. Her condition was a chronic one and she was weak and deconditioned. I scheduled her in the less busy times of the clinic and she showed improvements after just a few treatments. Her transfers became more automatic and less guarded. She was able to sit longer in a chair and she began walking for exercise on a daily basis.

She was educated on stabilization exercises to target her abdominal muscles. She was shown how to flatten the curve in her back while lying down. This was progressed to teaching her to lift and lower her foot with her back tilted. She was quickly progressed to straightening her knee and bending it with her back flat. This was described as rolling an egg gently under her heel. She was told to straighten her leg as far as possible without losing the tilt in her back or having her heel touch the table. She followed every direction she was given and she continued to see she was getting better.

A few weeks into her rehab I received a phone call from her referring physician. He complimented me on my patience and my progress with her. He believed she was a surgical candidate based on the severity of her injury and her failed response to pharmacological

intervention. He said the main reason for contacting me

was to ask about the nature of the treatments I had used to

get her better. He also wanted me to enlighten him on egg

rolls. I explained it was an abdominal stabilization

exercise that involved her sliding her heel while

maintaining it 1 ½ inches off the table. He laughed. I

wonder if he thought I was also serving her Wonton soup.

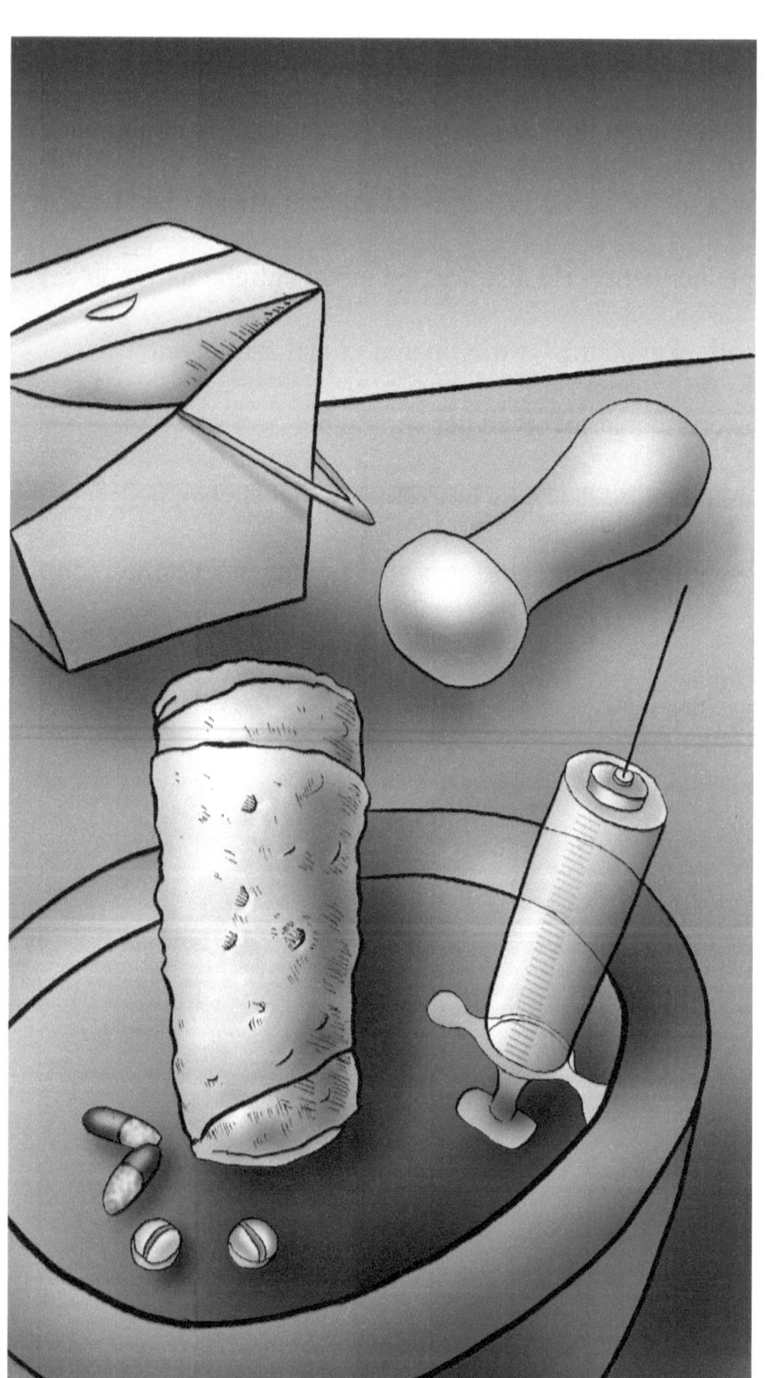

Chapter eight: Lessons they never teach in school

I felt confident taking exams in school. The material was thoroughly covered in lecture and lab. It was reinforced with homework assignments. I felt especially confident studying for the license exam when I realized I answered the majority of the questions correctly. Our curriculum prepared me for an exciting career. It did not, necessarily, prepare me for communicating with doctors, office managers, and bosses.

I opened a chart one day to see a script with a patient's name, a date, a doctor's signature, and the diagnosis of swimmer. In school it was drilled into our head that a medical diagnosis could come only from a medical doctor. As therapists we could only determine a physical therapy diagnosis. Swimmer. That was neither a body part nor was it a pathology.

We were also taught that medical doctors were the only clinicians able to determine weight bearing status. If patients entered our clinic with an assistive device the physician needed to indicate non weight bearing, toe touch weight bearing, partial weight bearing, weight bearing as tolerated, full weight bearing, etc. What amused me was a patient who came into the clinic last week with a script for shoulder tendonitis and the order of weight bearing as tolerated. I was expecting this patient to share that she was a performer with Cirque de Soleil and walking on her hands was part of her everyday routine. It turns out she was not employed by this company.

A few years into my profession I was working morning shifts in a facility and came across an office manager who did not behave professionally. She noticed there were unwashed dishes in the kitchen sink of the facility at 7:15 am, stomped onto the clinic floor, interrupted patient care, and raised her voice at me. "WE

DO NOT LEAVE DIRTY DISHES IN THE SINK.

EVERYONE USES THE KITCHEN. EVERYONE

SHOULD CLEAN THEIR OWN MESS."

I was never so embarrassed. I was embarrassed by her tone of voice, the content of her address, the lack of privacy, and her lack of respect. I was additionally embarrassed by her blaming me inappropriately. I, for once, was speechless. Patients, however, were not. They asked who she was and if that was how she spoke to everyone. They asked how we tolerated that type of behavior. They asked if she had taken classes on improving her management style.

When I had a break in my schedule I confronted her privately, introduced myself, and said that I was open to constructive criticism. I was not open to being accused of something I did not do. I was less open to being reprimanded in front of patients. I told her that if she had anything she ever wanted to discuss with me in the future that she should find a less public forum. She retired her megaphone for the next several years.

After several years of working in the field I interviewed with a large company. I had never worked with other therapists in a setting and was looking forward to treating among a variety of clinicians. I updated my resume and references, gathered salary information, dressed, and headed to the interview.

The manager was very casual. He reclined in a leather tilt back chair and glanced over my resume. He asked a few questions about my clinical ambitions; apathy punctuated his questions. I expected the interview to be cut short but he surprised me by handing me a copy of the benefit package. His apathy changed to passion as he described the continuing education classes, the medical benefits, the paid vacation days, and the 401K options the company offered. Before I knew it he had extended an offer and said he would like it if I joined their team. He felt I was a good candidate for the company and realized I had a lot to offer his patient population.

This reversal from apathy to passion to convincing me I was the best candidate took place in a brief amount of time. All that remained was the inevitable discussion of reimbursement. He asked what salary I desired and I asked what salary was in the company's budget. Upon hearing his answer I stood up, shook his hand, and turned for the door. He read my lack of interest in his offer and questioned why I chose not to negotiate. I thanked him for his time, but said had he offered something reasonable I would have begun negotiating. His offer was an insult and I did not feel like I could get anywhere with such a low and insulting figure. I thought it was best if I left like a lady and allowed him to continue his search for a more appropriate candidate.

Later that evening I shared this experience with a friend of mine. He thought I should have accepted the offer and responded with,"You've hired me Monday through Wednesday. What would you be willing to pay me if I work the rest of the week?" His alternate closing line was, "You've hired me part time; now let's talk about what you'd be willing to pay me if I work full time."

Although classes in school did not teach us how to communicate with insurance companies they did teach the importance of impeccable documentation. So I collected detailed histories, took thorough objective measurements, set functional goals, and reassessed progress. I justified the need for skilled care and showed the effectiveness of my interventions.

It was brought to my attention by an office worker that one date of service was not reimbursed. This puzzled me. Before reading the insurance company's explanation

I imagined there was no prescription for the date of service the treatment was given. I found this was not the case when I opened the chart. They were denying the evaluation, and a script for that date of service was in the chart. Their explanation was that the mechanism of injury was missing.

I read my typed report and came across insidious onset in the history. I decided no additional documentation would remedy this so I made a phone call to the insurance company. Once she pulled up the evaluation on her computer and refreshed her memory she inquired how the patient got injured. She asked on what date the injury was sustained. This is when I realized I was going to have a battle of the wits with someone who was unarmed.

The world of medicine is changing. Pharmaceutical companies are as subliminal as an EXIT sign illuminated red. They are telling patients to schedule visits with their physicians to discuss incontinence, erectile dysfunction, and clinical depression. WebMD has additionally helped patients identify (and recite) their symptoms. The differential diagnosis can be done in the comfort of the patients' bedroom. Doctors are prescribing medications to lessen muscle spasms, inflammation, and pain for patients with musculoskeletal complaints.

It is usually after patients fail to see relief from medication that their physician prescribes physical therapy. It must be after many failed medication prescriptions were written since their handwriting is barely legible! Perhaps doctors are unfamiliar with the field of physical therapy, the training of therapists, the modalities utilized, or the diagnoses which respond to treatment. I recall when a classmate of mine was unsure of the gender of a noun while completing a Spanish test he wrote illegibly. He figured the teacher would know the gender and whether the word needed to end with an O or an A. This may, in fact, be the origin of "Evaluate and Treat."

Each day I go in to the office I find a new challenge- deciding how to occupy my time when there are gaps in the schedule, deciding how to calmly and safely treat during busy hours, deciphering doctors' handwriting, deciphering my own handwriting, hypnotizing the parents of children so they refrain from playing twenty questions with me, and refraining from saying, "Then don't do that" when a patient says, "my arm only hurts when I do this."

Monday mornings are not just filled with follow up appointments of established patients, evaluations of new patients, and a means to accrue small increments for my bank account, but they also represent an opportunity for me to collect additional material for a second book.